At Issue

Can Diets Be Harmful?

Other Books in the At Issue Series

At Issue

Can Diets Be Harmful?

Amy Francis, Book Editor

GREENHAVEN PRESS
A part of Gale, Cengage Learning

GALE
CENGAGE Learning·

Farmington Hills, Mich • San Francisco • New York • Waterville, Maine
Meriden, Conn • Mason, Ohio • Chicago

GALE
CENGAGE Learning

Judy Galens, *Manager, Frontlist Acquisitions*

© 2016 Greenhaven Press, a part of Gale, Cengage Learning.

Gale and Greenhaven Press are registered trademarks used herein under license.

For more information, contact:
Greenhaven Press
27500 Drake Rd.
Farmington Hills, MI 48331-3535
Or you can visit our Internet site at gale.cengage.com

For product information and technology assistance, contact us at

Gale Customer Support, 1-800-877-4253
For permission to use material from this text or product, submit all requests online at www.cengage.com/permissions.

Further permissions questions can be e-mailed to permissionrequest@cengage.com.

Articles in Greenhaven Press anthologies are often edited for length to meet page requirements. In addition, original titles of these works are changed to clearly present the main thesis and to explicitly indicate the author's opinion. Every effort is made to ensure that Greenhaven Press accurately reflects the original intent of the authors. Every effort has been made to trace the owners of copyrighted material.

Cover photograph copyright © Images.com/Corbis.

LIBRARY OF CONGRESS CATALOGING-IN-PUBLICATION DATA

Can diets be harmful? / Amy Francis, book editor.
    pages cm -- (At issue)
  Includes bibliographical references and index.
  ISBN 978-0-7377-7394-1 (hardcover) -- ISBN 978-0-7377-7395-8 (pbk.)
  1. Reducing diets--Health aspects. 2. Diet in disease. I. Francis, Amy.
  RM222.2.C27537 2016
  613.2'5--dc23
                        2015026931

Printed in the United States of America
  1 2 3 4 5   20 19 18 17 16

Contents

Introduction

Most experts agree that the keys to achieving and maintaining human health include eating well, getting adequate rest, exercising, and managing stress. It sounds like a simple formula; however, how much and what to eat, how many hours of sleep to get, the best forms of exercise, and how to best take control of stress are all hotly debated. As a result, American consumers spend billions of dollars annually trying to figure out the best path to fitness. Whether perusing the latest health magazines, reading diet books, shopping for a new superfood, taking supplements, working out to exercise videos, streaming DailyBurn.com workouts, joining gyms, or attending yoga classes, the path to achieving wellness can be confusing and costly. Unfortunately, in many cases it can also be dangerous.

Recently CrossFit, a boot-camp style workout program, has come under scrutiny for a high number of cases of rhabdomyolysis. Rhabdomyolysis is a potentially life-threatening condition that results from the rapid breakdown of muscle cells that become toxic to the kidneys. Although previously seen primarily in people crushed in accidents or victims of electrical shock, it can also be caused by extreme muscle strain—particularly in untrained athletes, and this is where CrossFit has received its greatest criticism.

CrossFit attracts a large number of untrained participants. According to the CrossFit website, there are more than eleven thousand affiliated gyms and over one hundred thousand accredited CrossFit trainers across the globe. Introduced in 1995 by former gymnast and celebrity trainer Greg Glassman, CrossFit aims to "optimize fitness [with a regimen of] constantly varied, functional movements performed at high intensity in a communal environment that leads to health and fitness."[1] CrossFit confronted the allegations of its practices leading to rhabdomyolysis head on with efforts to build awareness within its community. In the *CrossFit Journal*, available at the organization's website, physician Michael Ray admits, "There is no way to separate the effectiveness of the training from all risk. A completely safe training program is doomed to produce only couch potatoes." However, Ray goes on to assure readers that "rhabdomyolysis is only occasionally seen in athletes" and "smart trainers can minimize the risk for their athletes."[2]

Eric Robertson, physical therapist and assistant professor of physical therapy at Regis University in Denver, Colorado, doesn't see it that way. In a 2013 *Huffington Post* article, he writes, "Rhabdomyolysis isn't a common condition, yet it is so commonly encountered in CrossFit that they have a cartoon about it, nonchalantly casting humor on something that should never happen."[3]

Brooke Ross experienced CrossFit for himself and wrote in *Livestrong*, "That rush and love of the gym is far from a bad thing, but the no-quit atmosphere has generated questions. And the mob mentality has taken the healthiest of behaviors and turned it into a growing danger." Although he concedes that "when done correctly, CrossFit is not inherently bad or ineffective," he adds that it isn't always done carefully and that inexperienced trainers can open a branded CrossFit gym after attending only a weekend seminar and taking a multiple-choice test. "Due to its extensive popularity," Ross continues, "many CrossFit gyms have diluted the system."[4]

1. "What Is CrossFit?" CrossFit.com, accessed June 6, 2015. www.crossfit.com/cf-info /what-is-crossfit.html.
2. Michael Ray, "The Truth About Rhabdo," *CrossFit Journal*, January 4, 2010. http:// journal.crossfit.com/2010/01/rhabdo-pdf.tpl.
3. Eric Robertson, "CrossFit's Dirty Little Secret," *Huffington Post*, September 24, 2013. www.huffingtonpost.com/eric-robertson/crossfit-rhabdomyolysis_b_3977598.html.
4. Brooke Ross "The Controversy Behind CrossFit," LiveStrong.com, April 14, 2015. www.livestrong.com/article/545200-the-fall-of-fitness.

Those looking for a less extreme exercise program might turn to yoga. With the focus on strength, flexibility, and harmony, yoga's benefits have been well documented and rarely questioned, but even this practice can result in significant injury as people flock to classes seeking health and wellness.

William J. Broad, writing of his own experience in *The New York Times*, explains, "In 2007, while doing the extended-side-angle pose, a posture hailed as a cure for many diseases, my back gave way.

"With it went my belief, naïve in retrospect, that yoga was a source only of healing and never harm."[5] He sought help from an expert, Glenn Black, who was a yoga teacher for nearly four decades. Broad writes:

> He gave me the kind of answer you'd expect from any yoga teacher: that awareness is more important than rushing through a series of postures just to say you'd done them. But then he said something more radical. Black has come to believe that "the vast majority of people" should give up yoga altogether. It's simply too likely to cause harm.[6]

Some of the factors Black points to that have increased the risks for practicing yoga would not be unfamiliar to the CrossFit crowd. Namely, yoga has become so popular that many instructors who set up studios lack proper training. Further, group sessions create a mob mentality in participants, forcing them to push themselves beyond their limits in an effort to keep up with others in the class or please the instructors. Broad continues, "According to Black . . . the biggest [factor] is the demographic shift in those who study it. Indian practitioners of yoga typically squatted and sat cross-legged in daily life, and yoga poses . . . were an outgrowth of these postures. Now urbanites who sit in chairs all day walk into a studio a

5. William J. Broad, "How Yoga Can Wreck Your Body," *New York Times*, January 5, 2012. www.nytimes.com/2012/01/08/magazine/how-yoga-can-wreck-your-body.html?_r=0.
6. Ibid.

couple of times a week and strain to twist themselves . . . despite their lack of flexibility and other physical problems."[7]

Most people trying out fitness programs in an effort to achieve a healthier lifestyle also seek out the best diet to accompany their efforts. The authors of the viewpoints on the following pages of *At Issue: Can Diets Be Harmful?* explore the benefits and potential hazards of several popular diet practices.

7. Ibid.

1

Low-Carb, High-Fat Diets Are Dangerous

Ben Greenfield

Ben Greenfield is author of the book Beyond Training *and writes a blog at* WellnessFX.

Diets that severely limit carbohydrates and include high amounts of fat can be damaging. Common problems with these diets include increased circulating triglycerides, high cholesterol, inflammation, and difficulty controlling blood sugar and thyroid levels. Anyone attempting a low-carbohydrate, high-fat diet should be monitored closely for these health concerns.

I personally have experimented with very low carbohydrate diets combined with extreme amounts of exercise . . . and have certainly noticed issues on my biomarkers . . . of which I would have never been aware if I weren't testing and tracking—and these were serious issues that threatened my long term hormonal health and longevity.

Four Pitfalls of Low-Carb, High Fat Diets

With low-carb, high-fat diets becoming more mainstream for everything from weight loss to physical performance, it's very important for you to be aware of common pitfalls with this diet—particularly pitfalls that may be directly quantified in your own blood biomarkers. Here are four dangers of a low-carb, high-fat diet that you need to be aware of:

1. Triglycerides. Not only are high levels of circulating triglycerides a good way to get fat fast, but studies have consistently linked high triglyceride levels with heart disease, heart attacks and stroke. Fructose is one quick way to elevate triglycerides, but this really doesn't seem to be an issue with high-fat, low-carbers. However, vegetable oils and animal fats can also raise triglycerides. The big issue here is that if these oils and fats have been exposed to high amounts of temperature and processing, triglycerides are getting dumped into your body chock full of free radicals. So if your high-fat diet includes a high amount of roasted seeds or roasted nuts, nut butters, heated oils such as heated coconut oil or heated extra virgin olive oil, barbecued meats or meats cooked at very high temperatures, then your triglyceride count is going to go up. You should have triglycerides that are less than 150mg/dL [milligram per deciliter], and a triglyceride to HDL [high-density lipoprotein, or good cholesterol] ratio that is no more than 4:1, but in most of the healthiest people I've worked with, triglycerides are under 100 and the triglyceride to HDL ratio is less than 2:1.

TSH [thyroid-stimulating hormone] will often elevate in a high-fat, low-carber—indicating potential for long-term thyroid and metabolic damage.

---

2. Inflammation. If you have high levels of cholesterol . . . which you probably do if you're eating a high-fat, low-carb diet, then you need to be worried if your HS-CRP [high-sensitivity C-reactive protein] levels (a primary marker of inflammation) . . . are above 1.0 mg/dL—even if you're a hard charging athlete. I like to see most people under 0.5 for CRP levels, and here's why: a high amount of inflammation in your body is going to make the cholesterol circulating in your bloodstream more likely to become oxidized, generating a high amount of heart and connective tissue-damaging free radicals. As a matter of fact, it's more dangerous to have high levels of cholesterol and high levels of CRP than low levels of cholesterol and high levels of CRP—even if your high levels of cholesterol are "healthy," big fluffy LDL [low-density lipoprotein, or bad cholesterol] particles, and not small, dense vLDL [very low-density lipoprotein] particles. In other words, no matter how many healthy fats you're eating, these fats may actually come back to bite you if you're creating high inflammation from too much exercise, not enough sleep, exposure to toxins and pollutants, or a high-stress lifestyle.

3. Glucose/HBA1C. Free-ranging glucose molecules in your bloodstream can adhere to cholesterol particles and cause those particles to remain in the bloodstream for long periods of time, since your liver can't properly process cholesterol when it has a glucose molecule attached to it. The longer cholesterol circulates in your bloodstream, the higher the likelihood that it will dig its way into an endothelial wall and potentially contribute to atherosclerosis or plaque formation. This is why it's so dangerous to eat a high-fat diet, but to also have your nightly dark chocolate bar, overdo it on the red wine, or have weekly "cheat days" with pizza, pasta, or sugar-laden ice cream. If you're going to eat a high fat diet, then you need to ensure your fasted blood glucose levels are staying at around 70–90mg/dL, and your hemoglobin A1C (a 3 month "snapshot" of your glucose) is staying below 5.5. If not, your high fat diet could actually be significantly hurting you.

4. Thyroid-stimulating hormone (TSH). Carbohydrates are necessary for the conversion of inactive thyroid hormone to active thyroid hormone, and if you're on an extremely strict low carbohydrate diet, then you may actually be limiting this conversion. Your TSH . . . is what tells your thyroid gland to "release more hormone," so your TSH rises when your thyroid gland is underactive, or conversion of inactive to active thyroid hormone is inadequate. A high TSH means that the pituitary gland is releasing its hormone to try to get the thyroid to respond and produce more thyroid hormone. Because of inadequate carbohydrates, TSH will often elevate in a high-fat, low-carber—indicating potential for long-term thyroid and metabolic damage. If I see a TSH above 2.0 or a trend towards higher values in someone who is testing repeatedly, I get worried—and prefer to see TSH at 0.5–2.0. Of course, this doesn't mean that you begin to shove carbohydrates indiscriminately down the hatch. However, it means that your high-fat, low-carb diet should include thyroid supporting foods rich in iodine and selenium . . . , such as sea vegetables and brazil nuts, and should also include carbohydrates timed properly, such as before, during or after workouts, when the carbohydrate is more likely to be utilized for energy and less likely to spike blood glucose levels.

2

High-Fat Diets Are Not Dangerous

Michelle Henry

Michelle Henry is a staff writer at the Toronto Star.

Calorie per calorie, fat is more rich in nutrients than carbohydrates and better at helping to satiate hunger pangs. The low-fat diet popularized in the 1950s originated from a scientist who misattributed the good health of a small group of Mediterranean people to their diet, which was low in animal fats. Unfortunately, the result of the low-fat diet decades later is an increase in dangerous health conditions such as diabetes and heart disease.

Nina Teicholz is hungry.

The American author, in town [Toronto, Canada] to promote her best-selling book, *The Big Fat Surprise*, is scanning the St. Lawrence Market's restaurants and food stands in search of fat.

She settles this recent March [2015] morning for the breakfast offering from Carousel Bakery, maker of Toronto's "most famous" peameal sandwich. It's about five slices of Canadian bacon—sadly, one of pork's leaner cuts—topped with a fried egg.

"Can you make it without the bun?" she says, calling the squishy white roll needless calories, before asking to see if they sold homogenized milk. Carousel sells 2 per cent or skim.

"You can't even get whole milk if you want it," she says, looking forlorn.

Teicholz, 49, is a lone, lipid-loving wolf in this low-fat, high-carb world.

Benefits of Fat in the Diet

Fats, saturated, cholesterol-filled and otherwise, are the unsung—more like, vilified—heroes of diet, she says.

And she should know.

The investigative journalist spent the last decade on a painstaking quest to take down the prevailing wisdom that demonizes these essential, health-dense nutrients, anointing them the villainous culprits behind heart disease.

Taking a magnifying glass to 80 years of scientific literature, Teicholz's gripping, 480-page book (Simon & Schuster) turns everything we know—or thought we knew—about diet, nutrition and healthy eating—on its head. For examples: red meat is more nutritionally dense than chicken, bacon is "better for your hips than a bagel," and an ounce of cheese is more nutritious than an apple, she says.

North Americans are fatter than ever ... despite following nutritional guidelines to eat mainly fruits, vegetables and whole grains.

The basis for our ardent belief in the "diet-heart hypothesis," she says, which has informed our views since the 1950s, rests on shaky ground. Soft, epidemiological science that never actually showed a link between eating fat and getting fat.

Much less dying from it.

In fact, she says, our demonization of fat—eggs, cream, the salty white marbling on the sides of our steaks—and fear of cholesterol has cost us lives, not saved them.

North Americans are fatter than ever, she says, despite following nutritional guidelines to eat mainly fruits, vegetables and whole grains.

Since Canada's low fat, high carb guidelines came out in 1992 (about 10 years after the U.S.) obesity and diabetes have risen.

"It's a tragedy," she says.

Teicholz sits down at a table near Carousel and unwraps the foil covering her breakfast. Using a fork and knife she cuts into her bun-less meal, a pile of streaky meat, edges curled with delicate yellow fat, and the egg yolk runs precipitously over the carnal heap.

"When I was a vegetarian this would have horrified me," she says, tucking in. "To generations of people the idea of eating fat is repugnant."

Teicholz spent her college years eating mostly vegetables and bagels, she says, always being hungry—and gaining weight. She lost those un-shakeable 10 pounds only as a restaurant columnist for a small newspaper, while gorging, she writes, on "pâte, beef . . . cream sauces . . . foie gras."

But her mission to find out why the pounds fell off in spite of her diet, began after she started researching a book on trans fats, the man-made molecules and unfortunate results of society's quest to replace the newly vilified lard, schmaltz, tallow, with something more acceptable.

Knee deep in the science, she was compelled to get her hands on almost every, original study out there. She said she realized there was a much bigger story there.

Origins of the Low Fat Hype

It originates in the early 1950s with a man named Ancel Keys, Teicholz writes in her book. The scientist believed he found, in part by studying a group of men on Crete, an island in Greece, that their good health and low rates of heart disease were due to a diet low in animal fats.

Powerful and outspoken, he launched a momentous public relations campaign against fat and, in the absence of any hard data his doom and gloom forecast "steamrolled over a sense of caution," she says, and turned the tides on nutrition—away from a focus on getting enough healthy foods and toward avoiding foods for "disease prevention," which continues today. Pouring over some of Keys' original studies, Teicholz realized his work was partly based on men who had been observing Lent—a time when Cretans dramatically reduced their consumption of meat and animal fats. From there, her narrative weaves through the diet crazes of the following decades, debunking fads and obsessions that have come and gone.

The Mediterranean diet, she shows, was based on problematic science, could never really be defined (each region from Italy to France to Greece eats different foods, in different proportions and diet became almost impossible to measure in a meaningful way), and olive oil, she writes, doesn't appear to be the nutritional panacea we had hoped.

---

100 calories of meat has 25 grams of protein—you'd have to eat about 666 calories of quinoa to get the same amount of protein.

She laments how [cardiologist Robert] Atkins—and his low-carb, high-fat diet—was incorrectly discounted. And how we've substituted nutritious foods—fat, beef, cream, eggs— with unstable vegetable oils, trans fats, carbohydrates.

And it's a challenge, she says, in this "high carb world of granola bars and chips" to find an alternative way of eating.

Organ meats, once the food served by dutiful mothers a few times a week, are near extinct. St. Lawrence Market butchers' counters gleam with brilliantly red, lean meats (primitive people used to chuck the sirloin to the dogs, Teicholz writes, because, lacking fat, it was less desirable)—to the detriment of our waistlines.

"Just think about it," she says, "100 calories of meat has 25 grams of protein—you'd have to eat about 666 calories of quinoa to get the same amount of protein."

Yet the fear of fat prevails.

And, she says, looms larger. The current, proposed U.S. dietary guidelines may recommend further lowering saturated fat, even though, she says, experts in charge are ignoring that top nutrition experts are taking a second look at the science used to condemn saturated fats in the first place. Not to mention, "the science is really not on their side."

Her critics say that her arguments are flimsy because she has "cherry picked" the studies she's used to make her point. Teicholz counters by saying all she did was analyze the flaws in their science—without positing a new hypothesis herself.

"I don't pretend that I know what causes diabetes, obesity and heart disease," she says.

There is a trickle of ever more vocal science and scientists who seem to agree with her concerns about dietary guidelines and are starting to voice their concerns (turns out dietary cholesterol is not linked with blood cholesterol in healthy people). But Teicholz isn't optimistic that change will come easily.

The clean eating food movements, led by the Michael Pollans [author, journalist, and food activist] and Mark Bittmans [*New York Times* food columnist], are hugely influential and tightly tied to robust environmentalism and our fears of destroying the planet.

She thinks it'll take U.S. congressional hearings on the matter to make power players realize nutritional policy is not based on sound science.

With that, Teicholz, thin and 5-foot-5 with wavy, shoulder length brown hair, looks down and contemplates her food for a moment.

If the "science" behind recommending low-fat diets for men was shoddy, she says, it was non-existent for women before governments started telling females to adopt the same, low-fat, high-carb dietary habits. Turns out, she says, women eating diets low in fat have an increased risk of heart disease.

Her belly full, hunger gone, Teicholz rests her fork and knife beside her leftovers. Eating fat is satiating, she says, so you don't have to think about calories.

"You just eat until you are full," she says. "It's liberating not to have to worry about that."

3

Paleo Diets Are Safe for Kids

Neely Quinn

Neely Quinn is a nutrition therapist and contributor to Paleo Plan.com.

Paleo is completely safe for children and is a much better option for children than the typical American diet. When using a paleo diet, some parents sometimes make the mistake of not giving their children enough carbohydrates, which are essential for growing children, but this pitfall can easily be avoided within the paleo parameters. Introducing children to the more varied, flavorful diet paleo provides when they are young may even give them a better appreciation for a diverse diet later.

I get this question more than I'd like to admit: Is eating Paleo safe for kids and babies? Allow me to answer a question with a better question: Is eating a Western diet safe for kids? No, it's not. And yes, eating Paleo is.

Why Wouldn't It Be?

The top reasons I'm assuming people think eating Paleo might be dangerous for their child or baby are these:

- Not enough nutrients

- Too much meat

- Not enough dairy (in other words, not enough calcium)

- Too much meat

- Not enough sugary snack foods?

Now, I could take this opportunity to make fun of people for being brainwashed by multi-gazillion-dollar marketing schemes and demented health "officials" into believing that Cocoa Puffs made with whole wheat (or whatever) are really the paragon of a good breakfast. Or for believing that milk from a *different species* is a vital part of a *human*'s diet. Or that sugary snacks are a good thing to give kids. Or adults for that matter. But I won't because I'm a nice person.

Paleo Is Safe

The straight answer to the question, again, is yes. Paleo is safe for children and babies alike. In fact, baby and children humans evolved eating Paleo the same as adult humans did for millions of years. Babies of hunter gatherers were given their mother's Paleo teat and then their mother's Paleo food to eat just like all the adults. Our ancestors didn't grow crops of soy, grains, and sugar just so they could make soy formula and soy crackers and Clif bars and rice cereal for their kids to suckle on before they changed them over to an "adult" diet of meat, fish, veggies, and fruits. You get my point. I strongly believe— ahem . . . KNOW—that Paleo is safe for kids and babies. They have all the digestive faculties in place to eat Paleo foods (aka "real" foods), and if you make it their only option *to* eat those foods, most kids won't hunger strike for very long until they figure out that being hungry sucks.

Traditional (and generally very healthy) people all over the world have given their children the same whole foods they eat from the get-go.

Having said that . . .
There are some things you should know.

Babies. For instance, a 6-month old's first solid food on his Paleo diet shouldn't be almonds or raw carrots or a big hunk of steak, either. Now maybe if that steak were blended . . .

And it shouldn't be super processed rice cereal like you're told by your doctor. If you read *Nutrition and Physical Degeneration* by Weston A. Price, you'll find that traditional (and generally very healthy) people all over the world have given their children the same whole foods they eat from the get-go. They give their babies spiced foods, fish (even raw fish— gasp!), fish eggs, miso soup, decaffeinated green tea, liver, eggs, fermented soy mash, rice mash, but always there's a solid protein source in there. Babies are better at digesting protein than carbohydrates before the age of 1, says Chris Kresser in his fantastic resource, *The Healthy Baby Code.*

Giving such young kids such flavorful foods begs the question: Would American kids like a wider array of foods if they weren't reared on bland food products like rice, crackers, and rice crackers?

Instead of rice cereal fortified with synthetic nutrients, start with, say, a cooked egg yolk and liver. If you're going Paleo yourself while you're breastfeeding, I wrote a blog post on what changes to make in your own diet when you're breastfeeding.

Kids. In terms of nutritional needs, kids are just like small adults, so they should be eating adult foods; not white foods with fake vitamins in them and pasteurized, lifeless cheese. I have to put my two cents in here and say that while this may be hard to implement in your household if you have kids who only want mac & cheese or else, it's better you do this now while you *can* sort of control what goes into their bodies. Be strong and be firm with them when you go Paleo. They'll get used to it and most likely start to like the foods you give them. Plus, your kids' waistlines and health will thank you for it later.

Kids and Carbs. Now, people do make mistakes when they put their kids on a Paleo diet, especially if those kids are active. Namely, parents put their little skinny kids on the same weight-loss Paleo menu that they're on. That is, low carb. GIVE YOUR KIDS ENOUGH CARBS! If they're hungry all the time, not growing properly, fatigued, nauseous, or not able to concentrate, you're A) probably not feeding them enough food in general and B) not feeding them enough carbs and fat. Meat and veggies are great, but just like an endurance athlete needs more carbs, so do your active, growing kids.

Western countries have the highest incidences of osteoporosis AND the highest consumption of dairy products. So what gives?

Sweet potatoes, squash, banana tapioca crepes, potatoes (yes, potatoes), and plenty of fruit will be your kids' friends. How much of all of those things really depends on your kid, but I'd shoot for a couple pieces of fruit a day and a small serving of sweet potatoes or one of the other starchy veggies I mentioned above with at least one meal per day. And don't skimp on those fatty, grass-fed cuts of meat. Kids need more fat than what comes on boneless, skinless chicken breasts. Give them the pork, the good cuts of beef, and some bacon. Coconut milk, coconut oil, olive oil, and avocados will also do the trick. The fat will give them energy.

Nutritional Density of Paleo Diet Compared to Western Diet

I did a comparison of the nutrient density of a typical Western diet and a typical Paleo diet. What I found was that Paleo won on all accounts except for calcium, sodium (not necessarily a bad thing), and vitamin D (because there's no fortified milk on the diet). I highly recommend you read that post [www.paleoplan.com] because I go into why that's not a bad thing more than I will go into it here. I'll only talk about calcium here because I know it's on your minds.

Calcium. Basically, Western countries have the highest incidences of osteoporosis AND the highest consumption of dairy products. So what gives?

In another blog post, I discussed how you need more than just calcium to build bones, and not as much calcium as your doctor may be over-recommending to you. Plus, it's important to know that calcium needs an alkaline environment to be absorbed properly, and when you're eating a ton of grains, dairy, beans, and sugar, you're creating an acidic environment.

Also, a lot of the calcium we ingest on a Western diet is bound to phytic acid, which is carried out of the intestines unabsorbed. You only get what you absorb.

Plus, on this particular day that I analyzed, the difference in calcium intake was only 97 mg, with Paleo coming in at 614 mg and the Western diet at 711 mg. Many cultures do well with way under those amounts. . . .

You can get a balanced array of calcium and other bone-building minerals from . . . wait for it . . . bones. Make some bone broth. It literally takes 1 minute of prep time to make it.

Meat. All I'll say about meat is that I've said it before. Your kid isn't going to die of rabbit starvation on a balanced Paleo diet. His kidneys won't fail (unless maybe he already has kidney disease), and he won't get gout. Read [my other posts] . . . for more information on why meat is not the devil. . . .

Having said that, though, you don't have to be pounding kilos of meat every day to call yourself Paleo. Some people just don't like meat that much. Fine. Eat less of it, more veggies, more fat, more fruit, and more nuts and seeds (sprouted and soaked, of course) and you'll be just fine.

From what I hear, parents are often surprised and delighted by how much their kids enjoy the meat and veggie recipes they make for them when they go Paleo. I think we underestimate kids' appetites for good, nourishing foods. Make some interesting, fun recipes like our Pork Tenderloin with Blueberry Sauce or the Coconut Salmon with Cream Sauce. You might be surprised!

4

Children Should Not Diet

Yoni Freedhoff

Yoni Freedhoff is a physician and assistant professor, faculty of medicine, at the University of Ottawa, in Canada.

Children should never be placed on a diet for weight loss. Weight loss is an adult problem, and the only way to help an obese child become healthier is to treat the parents. Children need a healthy, nurturing environment with nourishing food and plenty of time to engage in physical activity. Parents will do best to include the whole family in achieving this healthy lifestyle. Placing a child on a diet will only do more harm than good.

There's no debate that childhood obesity is a tremendous concern. I went to medical school in the early 1990s, and even just 20-odd years ago, what we know now as "Type 2 Diabetes" was still called "Adult Onset Diabetes." Not anymore. Nowadays kids with single-digit ages are coming down with what was once a disease of adulthood, and kids younger than 20 are being found to have the once-only-middle-age conditions of hardening of the arteries and fatty liver disease.

And of course it's not just medical problems these kids face. Studies on bullying behavior demonstrate kids with obesity are 2 to 3 times more likely to be bullied than their skinnier peers. Add that to the incredibly pervasive societal stigma against those with obesity, and it's hard to imagine that obesity isn't having a terrible impact on these kids' self esteem.

So if childhood obesity is so problematic, why wouldn't I suggest we treat it?

It's not the primary problem.

Kids Are Not the Problem

I'll repeat that. Childhood obesity is not the primary problem—or, to put it slightly differently, kids are not the problem. There's not an epidemic loss of willpower among 5 year olds, yet already by first grade, 1 in 3 children in America will be overweight or obese. The kids these days are no different than when we were kids. What's different is the world our kids are growing up in. Today's world is a Willy Wonkian dietary dystopia. It's an environment filled with nutritional misinformation, predatory advertising, misguided crop subsidies and aisles and aisles of ultra-processed boxes masquerading as food. It's a world where kids can't step on a blade of grass without being rewarded with a treat, where school fundraisers occur in Chick-Fil-A, and where Olympic gold medalists like Shawn Johnson, Chris Bosh, Apolo Ohno and Elana Meyers are busy helping to peddle chocolate milk to children as a "recovery" drink. (I've got to ask. What could these kids possibly be doing where for "recovery" they need a beverage [that] can contain 20% more calories and double the sugar of a full-sized Snickers bar?) Our world is the disease, and childhood obesity is just the symptom, and as a physician I know that while it's nice to treat symptoms, it's always more important to cure diseases.

What I teach the parents in my practice is to live the lives they want their children to live, and to never, ever, put an emphasis on doing so for weight-related reasons.

But I guess, given that we're not about to cure the world, it's fair to ask, "Shouldn't we treat the symptom?" Again, I draw on my training to answer. I was also taught that we shouldn't offer treatments without evidence to back up both the treatment's efficacy and its safety.

So is there a safe and effective diet for children? One that reproducibly, in a substantial and significant percentage of cases and in a sustainable manner, causes weight loss or prevents excessive gain? Unfortunately, the answer is plainly "no." And don't be lulled into thinking, "Yes, but we'll just have those kids eat less and exercise more." If it were that simple, do you think we'd still have a problem? Do you think these kids and society as a whole want to be bullied and victimized because of their weights? That they're choosing to purposely go out of their ways to "eat more and exercise less"? If you do, then I suppose you must also think playing the stock market is easy, because all you have to do is "buy low and sell high." But even if you're of the school that believes such an intervention or diet exists, is there data out there that tells me that administering that diet isn't going to irreparably damage a child's lifelong relationship with food, with their body image, or with their self-esteem?

No Safe "Diet"

I don't treat children in my practice, nor do I put my adult patients on prescriptive "diets." My oath as a physician to "do no harm" is one I take seriously, and given that I'm not aware of any diet plan for children that's actually proven to be safe, effective, and sustainable, picking up in my office where the schoolyard bullies left off, or suggesting that a parent do so, isn't something I'm comfortable recommending. And believe you me, as is evidenced by the story in *Vogue* [about Dara-Lynn Weiss who put her 7-year-old on a diet], a physician's expectation of parental action isn't necessarily what's actually going to happen once that parent gets his or her kid home. Moreover, I've got to ask, if full-grown, insightful, incredibly motivated, intelligent, mature adults with clearly weight responsive medical conditions struggle with long-term weight management and "dieting," how can anyone imagine that a young, innocent, immature, not-fully-developed-frontal-lobed child is going to be able to pull it off?

There is good news, though. There have been a number of studies now that demonstrate treating the parents can help the child. That's why I'll regularly recommend that, to treat individual cases of childhood obesity, we should be treating their parents and not the children. What I teach the parents in my practice is to live the lives they want their children to live, and to never, ever, put an emphasis on doing so for weight-related reasons (their own or their children's). It's about cultivating and nurturing healthy living behaviors—as regardless of a child's weight, every family, including those with skinny little rails, can benefit from more family-based cooking with whole, healthful ingredients, from active parents who carve out fitness time for themselves and their families, from less screen time and from more warmth. Those healthy living behaviors apply to every weight.

I've seen too many patients in my adult office who trace their struggle with food and weight back to a well-intentioned doctor and his or her straight talk about their "not so little anymore bellies"—or to a well-intentioned Mom or Dad who took them at an incredibly young age to Weight Watchers. Coupling that with the clear-cut fact that studies on parental feeding behaviors in kids demonstrate that being more restrictive backfires and leads to further dietary disinhibition and weight struggles, I can't in any good conscience recommend that children be placed on diets.

Until we have that reproducible, sustainable, effective and safe diet that we can prescribe with confidence, where we're assured we'll be doing no harm, I think we should stick to the parents, and also to rage against the world. The kids have it tough enough already.

5

The Typical American Diet Is Dangerous for Children

Amanda Chan

Amanda Chan was a staff writer for LiveScience Health and is the current editor for Yahoo Health.

Although it is tough for busy families to establish the habits that will lead to a healthy lifestyle for their children, it is critically important that they do so. Rates of childhood obesity and diabetes are skyrocketing even though these conditions are completely preventable. Planning meals to avoid convenience food and stocking the fridge with healthy snacks are two steps parents can take to help their children develop healthy habits to carry into adulthood.

Health experts say diets of children in the United States have deteriorated dramatically over the past two generations, leading to skyrocketing rates of obesity and diabetes, both of which put children at risk for other diseases and shorter lives. But as many parents know, eating healthy isn't always easy, especially when you're a mom of three growing boys, says Raleigh, N.C.-resident Michelle Morton.

Morton, who is a professional organizer, tries to buy only healthy foods from the grocery store for her 15-, 11- and 7-year-old sons. But it's challenging especially in the mornings, when she is trying to get all her kids out the door in time for school and not everyone is a fan of instant oatmeal.

"It's the time of the day when you have the least amount of time, so you're like, 'OK, so we had to eat Fruit Loops today,'" Morton told *MyHealthNewsDaily*. "That's been the hardest for me."

Morton tries to keep her kids from eating junk food by keeping only healthy snacks in the house, such as fruit, yogurt and cheese. She will let them have the occasional brownie or toaster pastry from time to time, but usually saves them for special occasions.

Today, 17 percent of all kids and teens are obese, which is triple the rate of one generation ago.

But as much as she encourages healthy eating, kids are always attracted to the junk, she said.

"They tend to always want that stuff, or at least that's the way it is at my house," Morton said. "It's always hard to try to find that balance to teach them to eat healthier and why to eat healthier, but at the same time not completely depriving them. They're just always attracted to it."

Health experts say the occasional treat is acceptable, as long as it is not in large quantities and not a daily ritual. But for kids who already have poor eating habits early in life, their sweet tooth is not wholly to blame—they are attracted to those foods because they learn at home and at school that they are OK to eat, said Eileen Kennedy, a pediatric psychologist at the Cleveland Clinic in Ohio.

Factors Contributing to Childhood Obesity

Today, 17 percent of all kids and teens are obese, which is triple the rate of one generation ago, according to the Centers for Disease Control and Prevention [CDC].

The American diet is likely not helping any. One study published in 2000 in the *American Journal of Clinical Nutrition* found the average American gets 27 percent of his or her total daily energy from junk foods. Most people don't realize how bad it's gotten. Some 90 percent of Americans reported eating a healthy diet in a recent *Consumer Reports* survey, though their weight and other factors suggest that's not the case.

"So many people think that what they're eating is healthy—diet frozen dinners, fat-free ice cream, 100-calorie pretzel packs. Or they say, 'I never eat fast food,' but that doesn't mean they're not eating a lot of other unhealthy things," Molly Kimball, a registered dietitian at Ochsner's Elmwood Fitness Center in New Orleans, said of that survey.

And this isn't a light topic: Obesity puts kids at higher risk for a slew of health issues, including diabetes, heart disease and even cancer. Already, about 151,000 children under age 20 have type 1 or 2 diabetes. And in the last two decades, type 2 diabetes—formerly known as adult-onset diabetes—has been reported among U.S. children and teens with increasing frequency, according to the CDC.

It's not necessarily that parents are trying to fatten their kids up with junk food and fast food, said Kennedy, the pediatric psychologist. Rather, it has to do with convenience and lack of meal planning.

"We have such a widespread availability of fast-food options, that it is just a flat-out convenience for very busy families," Kennedy told *MyHealthNewsDaily*.

There is also a general lack of importance placed on meal planning in American culture, she said.

"A common problem is that it gets to be 6 p.m., and Mom looks at Dad, and Dad's looking at the kids, and everyone is wondering what to eat that night," Kennedy said. If the solution is to drop by the fast-food restaurant around the corner, it becomes a habit and routine, she said. "You'll do it until you make an active decision that you won't do it as often." Instead, families should plan out their meals at the beginning of the week so that they can cook and eat together, if possible.

But as much as stress and lack of time account for some kids' poor eating habits, parents' submissiveness—the situations in which they allow kids to get their way, even with food—is also a big factor, Kennedy said.

Establishing Healthy Habits

To optimize healthy eating habits among kids, it's important the same food rules apply both at home and at school, Kennedy said. A parent can feed a child as much healthy food as she or he wants at home, but if the child is eating junk food for lunch at school, those efforts are wasted, she said.

A new study, presented this month [May 2011] at a meeting of the American Heart Association, showed that school interventions during sixth grade helped to keep kids' cholesterol and resting heart rate down four years later.

The intervention included teaching kids to eat more fruits and vegetables and less fatty foods, to choose less sugary beverages, to exercise at least 150 minutes a week and to spend less time in front of the television and computer.

Researchers picked middle-school students for the study, because that is the age when kids start to make their own choices in terms of their activities or what they are eating, said study researcher Dr. Elizabeth A. Jackson, assistant professor of internal medicine at the University of Michigan.

"It's a great time to give them some independence in a healthy way instead of a negative way," Jackson told *MyHealthNewsDaily*.

Eating healthfully can be hard especially in lower-income neighborhoods where there aren't as many healthy food options or extracurricular physical activities offered at schools, she said.

"It's really a multilevel kind of environmental type phenomenon that pushes kids toward more sedentary behavior and more poor food choices," she said.

The High-Calorie American Diet Has Created a Health Crisis

Chris Woolston

Chris Woolston is a science, health, and travel writer.

The typical Western diet is the exact opposite of what experts say we should be eating, and as a result Americans are suffering from an obesity health crisis. Part of the problem is that Western culture encourages convenience foods and large portion sizes. High-calorie, quick snacks and meals win out over meal planning, cooking at home, and consuming sensible portions. People need to take control of their diet and make the healthy choices that will help them live healthy lives and avoid diet-related health conditions.

What's wrong with the typical American diet? This is what the experts have to say:

"Too many calories," says Marion Nestle, PhD, MPH [Master of Public Health], Professor of Nutrition and Food Studies at New York University.

"Too many calories," asserts Melanie Polk, registered dietitian and former director of nutrition education for the American Institute of Cancer Research.

Barbara Gollman, a registered dietitian who used to be the spokesperson for the American Dietetic Association, weighs in with her own theory: "Too many calories."

Chris Woolston, "What's Wrong with the American Diet?" *HealthDay*, March 11, 2015.

Perhaps it's time to stop talking about fatty foods and admit that we simply eat too many calories. Twenty-five years ago, the average American consumed about 1,850 calories each day. Since then, our daily diet has grown by 304 calories (roughly the equivalent of two cans of soda). That's theoretically enough to add an extra 31 pounds to each person every year. Judging from the ongoing obesity epidemic, many Americans are gaining those pounds—and then some.

Take the latest national surveys on weight. More than 68 percent of all Americans are considered overweight or obese, according to the Centers for Disease Control and Prevention. (This means they have a body mass index greater than 25.)

But calories don't tell the whole story. To truly understand what's wrong with the American diet, you have to know how we manage to consume all those calories. There are two possible ways to go overboard: You can eat too many calorie-dense foods, or you can eat too much food or beverages in general. Many people choose to do both.

Our fondness for fast food is taking a particularly heavy toll. Although the federal government recommends that we have at least two to five cups of fruits and vegetables a day, for example, surveys show that the average American eats only three servings a day, and 42 percent eat fewer than two servings a day.

Here's a closer look at our love affair with calories—and the health crisis it has created.

Studies have shown that a high-fat, low-nutrient diet increases the likelihood of colon cancer, diabetes, and a host of other ailments.

The Western Diet

Of course, there is no single American diet. We all have our individual tastes, quirks, and habits. Still, experts see clear patterns in our food choices. In fact, most American diets fall into one of two broad categories: "Western" or "prudent."

The prudent diet is a nutritionist's dream. People in this category tend to eat relatively large amounts of fish, poultry, cruciferous vegetables (i.e. cabbage and broccoli), greens, tomatoes, legumes, fresh fruits, and whole grains. They also skimp on fatty or calorie-rich foods such as red meats, eggs, high-fat dairy products, french fries, pizza, mayonnaise, candy, and desserts.

The Western diet is the prudent diet reflected in a carnival mirror. Everything is backwards: Red meat and other fatty foods take the forefront, while fruits, vegetables, and whole grains are pushed aside. In addition to fat and calories, the Western diet is loaded with cholesterol, salt, and sugar. If that weren't bad enough, it's critically short on dietary fiber and many nutrients—as well as plant-based substances (phytochemicals) that help protect the heart and ward off cancer.

Put it all together and you have a recipe for disaster. In a 12-year study of more than 69,000 women, published in the *Archives of Internal Medicine*, a Western diet was found to significantly raise the risk of coronary heart disease. Other studies have shown that a high-fat, low-nutrient diet increases the likelihood of colon cancer, diabetes, and a host of other ailments.

The Western diet is nothing new. The typical American family in the 1950s was more likely than we are to sit down to a meal of pork chops and mashed potatoes than stir-fried tofu and broccoli. So why has the obesity epidemic exploded in the last 20 years? It's a matter of size. "Twenty years ago, the diet wasn't as varied as it is today, and people didn't eat nearly enough fruits and vegetables," Gollman says. "But the portions were more in line with what people really need."

From bagel shops to family restaurants to vending machines to movie theater concession stands to the dining room table, our meals and snacks are taking on gargantuan proportions. "Everyone in the food industry decided they had to make portions larger to stay competitive, and people got used to large sizes very quickly," Nestle says. "Today, normal sizes seem skimpy."

The hyperinflation of our diet is especially obvious away from home. "Look through the window of any of the big chain restaurants, and you'll see huge platters of food coming out of the kitchen," Polk says. One of those platters could easily pack 2,000 calories, enough to last most people all day.

The Convenience Culture

Despite our national obsession with weight loss, the obesity epidemic continues to be a national health concern. The human craving for fats and sweets will never go away, and it's getting easier than ever to satisfy those cravings. With 170,000 fast-food restaurants and 3 million soft-drink vending machines spread across the country, huge doses of calories are never far away—especially when those soda machines are sitting right in the middle of public schools.

Fatty, unbalanced, and oversized: That, in a nutshell, is the American diet.

In 1978, for example, the typical teen-age boy in the United States drank about seven ounces of soda a day, according to *Fast Food Nation* author Eric Schlosser. Today, he drinks nearly three times that much, getting a whopping 9 percent of his daily calories from soda. Teenage girls are close behind.

Perhaps not surprisingly, studies show that childhood obesity has hit epidemic proportions over the last few decades. The main culprits, according to experts: high-fat foods, sodas, and too little exercise.

Fatty, unbalanced, and oversized: That, in a nutshell, is the American diet. But it doesn't have to be your diet. "People think eating healthy is a difficult task, but small things make a big difference," Polk says. "You just have to employ some important strategies. It's called taking charge."

If you eat more than four meals away from home each week, you can start by making healthy choices as you dine. "As we eat at restaurants more and more, we have to take control of these outlandish meals," Polk says. Order foods that have been baked, steamed, or grilled instead of deep-fried. Have your salad dressing or other fatty toppings served on the side, and if mayonnaise isn't low-fat, skip it entirely. Consider ordering a salad and an appetizer instead of an entree. If you do order an entree, plan to take at least half of it home with you.

No matter where you eat, try to stick to a few basic guidelines. The amount you should eat depends on your age and activity level—teenage boys and men need to eat more than young children, for example. Aim for three to eight ounces of bread, cereal, rice, or pasta each day, the more whole grains the better. This isn't quite as daunting as it sounds—one cup of rice counts as two ounces, and a single slice of bread counts as one ounce. Two to five cups of fruits and vegetables each day will give you fiber and vital nutrients; if you're using a plate, try to cover half of it in produce. (One serving is a medium piece of fruit, a half cup of chopped fruit, a half cup of chopped vegetables, or a cup of fresh greens.) Taken together, fruits, vegetables, and grains can satisfy your hunger and fuel your body without blowing your calorie budget.

Meat isn't forbidden, but try to think of it as a complement to your meals, not the main attraction. According to the U.S. Department of Agriculture (USDA) food pyramid, you only need two servings (up to six and a half ounces) from the "meat group" each day. The group includes meat, poultry, fish, dry beans, eggs, and nuts. It goes without saying that six ounces of salmon, pinto beans, or chicken breast is preferable to six ounces of marbled steak (a serving of meat, by the way, should be about the size of a deck of cards).

Much of the advice can be boiled down to one word: moderation. By eating different foods from every part of the pyramid and watching your portion size, you can make your own personal American diet healthy and nutritious. We have more choices and more temptations than ever before, but ultimately, we also have the final say over what we eat. Take control, and enjoy.

7

Low-Calorie Diets Create Health Problems

Shan Guisinger

Shan Guisinger is a clinical psychologist specializing in the treatment of eating disorders.

Attempting to stick to a low-calorie diet actually increases the risk of developing obesity, diabetes, or an eating disorder. Dieting, particularly calorie-restrictive diets, puts people at risk for these conditions as humans are biologically predisposed to prevent starvation. Rather than attempt to count calories, people should simply eat small, frequent meals and accept the genetically determined size and shape of their bodies.

Because our ancestors were adapted to survive famine, very low calorie diets can make dieters more obese, trigger eating disorders, and increase the risk of obesity and diabetes for their children and grandchildren.

Our bodies bring hundreds of millions of years of evolution to the problem of famine. In the *New York Times Magazine* (January 1, 2012) Tara Parker-Pope reported research showing that biological mechanisms cause dieters to regain their lost weight. This seems to come as a surprise to Parker-Pope, but her conclusion, that diets fail over the long-term, is not news. In the last decade review articles in *Nature, Science,* the *New England Journal of Medicine,* and *The American Psy-*

chologist have concluded that diets are not the answer to obesity because over the long term the body responds to weight loss by storing more fat.

Diets do work initially. We seem to be able to tolerate and even enjoy short-term weight loss. This makes sense; when our ancestors lived as hunter-gatherers, there were times when the body needed to quiet hunger pangs and focus on migrating or getting by until spring. But over the longer term the body tries to return to its pre-diet weight, and because energy regulation is under neuroendocrine control, weight cannot be permanently controlled by conscious effort.

Diets and Genetics

Information that food is scarce leads to changes in gene expression that alter every level of the body's powerful energy regulation system. A network of chemical switches, collectively known as the epigenome, work like a volume knob on the gene, by making it easier or more difficult for the cell's protein-making machinery to read them. This allows organisms to respond to environmental conditions. Epigenetic chemical markers serve as a layer of genetic control on top of the DNA sequence—thus their name "epi" means "above." The amount of food and regularity of eating feeds back to the genes via these epigenetic pathways. Some genetic mechanisms are hundreds of millions of years old. For example, one obesity gene, FTO, that is up-regulated by dieting in humans plays a similar role in energy utilization in yeast.

You could be sitting at a banquet, but if you restrict calories your hypothalamus figures you live with famine.

Genes can be permanently altered by the conditions an organism encounters. One extreme diet in adolescence can set up an individual for weight struggles the rest of his or her life. In a study of 14,972 American adolescents followed over three years, [A.] Field and colleagues found dieters gained more weight than non-dieters, even when researchers controlled for age, gender, BMI [body mass index], calorie intake and physical activity. In other words, the diet made the body more efficient at using energy and storing it. Adolescents who were underweight or normal weight were as susceptible to weight gain as those who were overweight.

A recent review of 31 long-term diet plans published in *The American Psychologist* found dieters gained more weight than nondieters. The evidence convinced the authors to advise Medicare and Medicaid policymakers that diets are counterproductive for weight control. [T.] Mann and colleagues wrote, "Even in studies with the longest follow-up times (of four or five years postdiet), the weight gain trajectories did not typically appear to level off. It is important for policymakers to remember that weight regain does not necessarily end when researchers stop following study participants."

For hundreds of millions of years the biggest danger facing animals was starvation and our bodies are exquisitely sensitive to that threat. Deep in the brain an ancient region called the hypothalamus monitors nutritional status and manipulates our appetite to get us the things we need. The hypothalamus gets its information about protein, sugar, fat, salt and water levels from sampling the blood, not from the conscious mind. You could be sitting at a banquet, but if you restrict calories your hypothalamus figures you live with famine.

When starving, the hypothalamus turns up hunger so we can think of little but food; it keeps satiety (fullness) signals low so that when food becomes available we can gorge, and it quiets the part of the brain responsible for self-restraint. One study published this fall [2011] in the *New England Journal of Medicine* found that hunger signals were still significantly elevated a full year after obese people went on an eight-week, very low calorie diet. The dieted body can lower metabolic rate up to 40%, slow transit time in the gut to extract more of the nutrients from food, and divert calories from energy into fat storage.

Starvation turns up the brain's rewards for eating to motivate food searches. Indeed, street drugs exploit reward systems that first evolved to insure that animals eat. For example, when starving opiate receptors are amplified so that eating pasta can feel like an addict's fix. Increased cannabinoid receptors make food taste like you're stoned. Dopamine, the brain chemical that plays a key role in orgasm and in addiction, surges when a starving person eats.

Researchers believe that the same adaptations that allow individuals to utilize calories more efficiently under conditions of food scarcity contribute to diabetes and obesity when food is plentiful.

One popular explanation for the obesity epidemic is that people have learned to associate eating with a reward. Parker-Pope quotes Rena Wing, a psychiatry professor at Brown [University], "We've taught ourselves over the years that one of the ways to reward yourself is with food." But people do not have to learn that eating is rewarding. Wing's naïve statement illustrates the widespread ignorance of the body's powerful energy regulation system, even among weight loss experts.

Children and Low-Calorie Diets

Scientists are finding that a very low calorie diet can also put our children and even grandchildren at higher risk for obesity and diabetes. Scientists first began to suspect that a mother's diet could program her adult child for obesity by studying people born to mothers who were pregnant during the Dutch Hunger Winter of 1945. [Adolf] Hitler cut off food to Holland and thousands died of starvation. Women who were pregnant gave birth to infants that were smaller than normal, but epigenetic modifications prepared the children to survive famine by increasing their appetites and ability to store fat.

The offspring of rats who were undernourished during pregnancy also become obese adults. Rats turn out to be wonderful exemplars of human obesity and eating disorders. Rats and humans evolved in similar ecological niches as omnivorous, opportunistic nomadic foragers and the hypothalamus is structurally preserved through mammalian evolution. Like most animals, rats maintain a healthy weight in the wild and in the lab when allowed a normal diet and activity. But if given a rich diet and no exercise they will gain more weight. If they are dieted and then given a rich diet they become obese.

Epidemiologists believe epigenetic modification could help explain the obesity epidemic in China, where the children of mothers who starved during Mao's Great Leap Forward [1958–1960] are now obese in middle-age. Researchers believe that the same adaptations that allow individuals to utilize calories more efficiently under conditions of food scarcity contribute to diabetes and obesity when food is plentiful. Since the children grew up with plenty to eat, they become overweight and at greater risk of developing diabetes. Pregnant mothers who follow a very low calorie diet may signal the fetus that it will live with famine.

Epigenetic adaptations to famine can be passed down at least two generations. The daughters of women who were pregnant during the Dutch famine gave birth to babies who were also smaller than average. Famine experienced by boys can even influence their grandchildren's health. The Överkalix Cohort Study looked at the progeny of men in northern Sweden who had lived through a severe famine during their preadolescence. Researchers found increased risk of diabetes, obesity and cardiovascular disease for the men, their children and grandchildren. Very low calorie diets also cause eating disorders. All the human eating disorders can be triggered in rats by restricting calories. If starved or if food is limited to one hour a day rats spontaneously develop anorexia behaviors where they ignore their food to run on a wheel. In the wild this activity would have helped them find food, but in the lab cage they can run themselves to death. Researchers have found that anorexia behaviors are triggered in both rats and humans by declining fat stores. Gorging, which is part of bulimia and binge eating disorder is a normal response to starvation. If you give stress dieted rats access to sugar water, they binge eat.

Eating Disorders

Evolutionary adaptations to survive famine give form to the symptoms of anorexia nervosa, bulimia, and binge eating disorder. I believe eating disorders only make sense in the light of evolution, but most popular theories are derived from patients' explanations of their behavior. Although only 2% of our brain is conscious, it tries to make sense of the actions of the other 98%—including activities of the hypothalamus—in psychological terms.

In the 1960s fewer people dieted and 15% of the population was obese and eating disorders were rare. Marilyn Monroe, wore a size 12. As weights of models and film stars began to decline, more people dieted and we became a nation obsessed with food. Today models are often a size 0, nearly 50% of the population dieted in the past year, eating disorders have tripled, and obesity rates have risen to 34%.

We should eat in a way to convince our bodies that they no longer, and will never again, live with famine. That means never go on a reduced calorie diet.

Given the evidence of diets inefficacy and perniciousness we should be asking, *Why is the diet industry allowed to promote the very behavior that leads to greater obesity and to eating disorders?*

According to a study of everyday stress, by the time they are middle-aged both men and women list unhappiness with their weight as their number one daily stressor, people who despise themselves for their failure to maintain their ideal weight often project their disdain onto those who are fatter. Prejudice against fat people is rationalized by the belief that fat is unhealthy, but for the middle 60% of the weight distribution there is no correlation between health and weight. In fact, people who are overweight, but not obese, have a lower risk of death than normal weight or underweight people.

Genetic studies have found that weight is as heritable as height, yet many people wake up everyday hating their weight and scorning those who are fatter. Although tallness and thinness are both valued, there isn't widespread contempt of short people; height is seen as beyond the individual's control. If a short person woke up every day hating her height we would question her sanity and values.

Is there no solution then to obesity and eating disorders? Actually there is. We should eat in a way to convince our bodies that they no longer, and will never again, live with famine. That means never go on a reduced calorie diet. Most people should eat more frequent, smaller meals beginning with breakfast. We should eat a diet closer to the one humans evolved with. There are no naturally occurring sweet fats or processed carbohydrates and our bodies don't regulate as well with them. Follow [First Lady] Michelle Obama's advice to substitute water for soft drinks, and increase fruits and vegetables. It is easier to do if you stop dieting. Find some physical activities you enjoy and make time for them. And then pray for the grace to accept the body you have.

8

Detox Diets Are Harmful

Jill Richardson

Jill Richardson is the author of Recipe for America: Why Our Food System Is Broken and What We Can Do to Fix It *and founder of the blog* La Vida Locavore.

Detox diets and cleanses are not the health fixes their advocates proclaim them to be. Although weight loss often results from following a detox diet or going through a cleanse diet, the weight loss is the result of lost fluids and muscle mass. Further, these diets can lead to sluggish metabolism and laxative dependence, which can hinder future weight loss efforts. The body is very effective at ridding itself of toxins and these diets only interfere with the body's natural processes and are harmful to one's health.

After a month-long national eating binge in December, Americans wake up on January 1 hoping to wipe the slate clean and start fresh in the new year. How do we undo the damage we did to our bodies with all of the eggnog and Christmas cookies? Many hit the gym. Others decide it's time to detox.

Detox diets, sometimes known as cleanses or flushes, are often advocated as ways to purge the body of toxins. Some even claim to help you expel gallstones. But do these extreme diet regimes actually work? Or are they, in fact, ineffective and even dangerous?

Cleanses and flushes tend to take two main forms. The first, known as the Master Cleanse or the lemonade diet, instructs people to fast for 10 days while consuming only a special lemonade made with lemon juice, water, maple syrup, and cayenne. Additionally, one must take laxatives before bed and then drink salt water in the morning to induce a bowel movement.

The second, often called a liver flush or a liver and gallbladder flush, originates from the work of Randolph Stone. Stone was a natural medicine doctor who developed what he called Polarity Therapy in the 1940s. There are many variations of Stone's liver flush around today, but most involve the same main components.

Some versions begin with a fast during which one consumes only apples and apple juice. Some also include instructions to drink water mixed with Epsom salts (a laxative). But all of the variations include two main components: drinking a mixture of lemon juice, garlic juice and olive oil followed by an herbal tea. The herbal tea usually consists of flax seeds, fenugreek and fennel seeds, but may also include other ingredients like burdock root and peppermint. Last, some versions of the flush say to eat a special diet for the rest of the day. This procedure may be repeated for a period of days, and some versions instruct one to do the flush at regular intervals throughout the year.

Really pushing the body hard to do things that are physically stressful . . . can really stress your vital organs.

Flushes' Laxative Effects

What does one achieve with such a strange regimen of foods? Let's just say you'll spend some quality time with your toilet if you give this flush a try. Most of the core ingredients in the flush are laxatives or diuretics. Some Web sites claim you will actually excrete up to 2,000 gallstones with this flush.

As it turns out, you won't excrete gallstones at all, although the flush will cause you to excrete what looks like little green "stones." So what are they? "Saponified olive oil," answers clinical herbalist Rosalee de la Forêt. Remember, you just drank a large amount of olive oil and lemon juice, and it has to come out the other end. The olive oil actually turns into soap inside your body. The soap absorbs bile, turning it green—although it's been shown that when someone drinks red dye along with the liver flush mixture, the stones will be red on the inside.

When asked about the effects of Master Cleanse and liver flushes, experts like De la Forêt, herbalist Sean Donahue and registered dietitian Melinda Hemmelgarn are surprisingly consistent with one another—and frustratingly vague.

Donahue, who teaches at the School of Western Herbal Medicine at Pacific Rim College, feels that the impacts of these regimes "vary a lot according to the person's general health," adding that, "often people who are looking to these solutions are people who are already depleted. Really pushing the body hard to do things that are physically stressful for it under those conditions at the very least kind of saps your vital reserves and at the worst can really stress your vital organs."

Hemmelgarn concurs, saying, "Everyone is an individual in terms of how they might feel after following these kinds of dietary restrictions. A dietitian would want to ask their clients about other conditions they might have, what kinds of medications they're taking, etc. What I can tell you is at the very least this kind of dietary restriction won't provide needed daily nutrients."

De la Forêt adds that she too would begin by asking a patient what symptoms they are experiencing and why they feel the need to do a "cleanse." She says, "In Ayurveda and traditional Chinese medicine, fasting and cleansing and purging do play an important role, but we always want to look at the individual person and create a plan that works for them."

In other words, there is no one-size-fits-all magic bullet to better health.

Yet, one [web]site advertising a liver flush claims, "The Polarity Cleansing Diet is a safe cleansing and health-building regime. It is a diet that you and your clients can use without experienced professional supervision. It can be used for health building under almost any circumstance, by any constitutional type, and at any time of the year."

Both Western and alternative medicine sometimes do advocate extremely restricted diets, fasts or purges using laxatives—but often not for general, all-purpose detox. For example, a patient may receive instructions to fast and take laxatives to empty his colon prior to surgery or a colonoscopy. Or a doctor might tell a migraine patient to eat a very restricted diet, slowly reintroducing foods one at a time until she identifies which food, if any, triggers migraines.

It's very common that people dramatically lose weight during these fasts which they then put on very easily after the cleanse ends.

The Master Cleanse and liver flush each promise amazing health benefits—often along with scary descriptions of the toxins that accumulate in one's body without doing a cleanse. For example, a site advocating the Master Cleanse promises it will, "not only make you healthier, it will also lead to increases in energy levels, make you more able to get rid of bad habits, cleanse the body of harmful toxins, and promote weight loss through the increased energy levels and smoother, stronger metabolism rate that will accompany it."

Damaging, Not Cleansing, Results

But a starvation diet like Master Cleanse does not actually deliver on those results, explains De la Forêt. "Some people do these things as a weight-loss thing. In Hollywood, the Master Cleanse has been touted as a way to lose a lot of weight. And of course they will, because it is a starvation diet." But, she continues, "What you're also doing is losing muscle mass because you have no protein in your diet. And one of the most important muscles is the heart, so the longer you fast, the more harm can be done to the heart."

As for the claim that you will come out of the fast with a stronger metabolism, she says the opposite is true. "Whenever we go into starvation mode, then we are also slowing down our metabolism and so it's very common that people dramatically lose weight during these fasts which they then put on very easily after the cleanse ends." She adds that a starvation diet like this can cause gallstones.

Hemmelgarn also worries about the laxatives used in these cleanses, which often contain senna leaf, that could cause adverse health effects—particularly when used for an extended period of time. Her advice on herbal laxatives? "*Avoid* them."

Herbalists are cautious about prescribing laxatives unless they are truly needed to treat short-term constipation. Donahue explains his views on laxative use, saying "It all depends on how you're doing it. If someone has been chronically constipated, then there can be some benefit to gently helping the body along." As an herbalist, his goal is to "help return to normal elimination."

This could include recommending bitter herbs like dandelion greens, which gently stimulate secretion of digestive juices, or helping patients make dietary changes. "But," says Donahue, "in terms of doing things that really force the body to eliminate" using laxatives when one isn't suffering from constipation in the first place? "Those can really do real damage."

"Often a person with chronic constipation has already had some damage to their gut lining," he notes, and many herbal laxatives work by irritating the gut lining. (Not a good thing if it's already damaged.) Even for those with a healthy gut lining, "most laxatives, even herbal laxatives, can create dependence in a very short period of time." As Donahue puts it, "The body realizes that something else can do this for me, this isn't where my energy needs to go."

The most serious danger both De la Forêt and Donahue see in the liver flush is that someone may actually dislodge a real gallstone (not the fake gallstones one produces and excretes during the flush). "If [a gallstone] gets stuck in your gallbladder duct, that's emergency surgery. So a lot of people in the know tell people not to do these flushes," says De la Forêt.

If fasting and drinking lemonade for 10 days isn't the way to detox your body then, how does one go about detox? The answer is simple, boring and straightforward: Eat right, exercise and get enough sleep.

De la Forêt explains that our body already has excellent detox mechanisms built in to eliminate both toxins and metabolic wastes. "When all of those are operating optimally, our body is functioning at a great level and all of those metabolic wastes are being taken care of naturally." She adds that our bodies are so "complex and amazing" that our own natural detox mechanisms are way more effective than a lemonade fast or liver flush.

Both she and Donahue note that our natural detox mechanisms can stop working properly—perhaps one becomes constipated, for example—so an herbalist will help a patient find a way to "support that natural function of our body to facilitate the elimination of metabolic waste."

Keep Toxic Loads Low

Supporting the body's natural detox mechanisms begins with putting the right nutrients in your body so that it can work. Avoiding known and preventable toxins is another step in the right direction. Hemmelgarn provides a list of advice for those looking to keep their bodies' toxic loads as low as possible:

1. Drink filtered tap water. (She adds, "This is not a recommendation to buy bottled water. It's a recommendation to

pay attention to where your water comes from and work to protect public water systems from pollutants and polluters.")

2. Read labels and avoid genetically engineered ingredients. Unless the label says "USDA [US Department of Agriculture] organic," any corn, soy, canola, and sugar (from beets, not sugar cane) comes from a genetically engineered crop. They have never been tested for long-term safety. While you're at it, tell the FDA [US Food and Drug Administration] you want GMO foods [genetically modified organisms] labeled as such. Join the justlabelit.org movement.

3. Choose local and organic foods whenever you can, and remember that the word "natural" on a label means little.

4. Ideally, meat and dairy products should be certified organic and pasture-raised.

5. Avoid foods and beverages in plastic packaging.

6. Avoid canned foods unless you can be sure the manufacturer does not use BPA [bisphenol-A]-lined cans. Go with glass instead.

7. If you drink soda (diet or regular), quit.

8. Get at least 30 minutes of physical activity every day, but do what you enjoy.

9. Practice meditative breathing.

10. Get adequate sleep.

11. Advocate for universal healthcare, clean environmental, agricultural and energy policies. A toxic environment can overburden even the cleanest diets.

Hemmelgarn's list is nearly identical to the recommendations provided by De la Forêt and Donahue. De la Forêt comments on a few of these tips, saying that, "Exercise is one of our best detox methods—it helps clean out all of the nooks and crannies."

As an herbalist trained in traditional Chinese medicine, she provides some additional advice. "I really believe in herbs and foods with a lot of antioxidants. Eating bitter foods or taking digestive bitters with all foods can help stimulate digestion," she says. This helps one both absorb foods better and get rid of wastes. Traditional Chinese medicine also advocates eating and living seasonally, which means supporting our bodies by eating more warm, dense, and heavy foods during the winter, and sleeping more. "This is the worst time of year to eat cold foods and do starvation diets," says De la Forêt. "Prolonged fasts consuming only foods like juices and raw foods are really damaging this time of year."

Additionally, she notes that, "In herbalism we look at if someone is experiencing symptoms of excess or deficiency. A greater percentage of the population that I see have deficiency symptoms: tired, weak, sluggish digestion, cold body temperature." Fasts or purges are "the last thing these people need." Instead, "they need building, nourishing [food] to help support their energies. And these are the people I see who really want to do these cleanses because they feel sick."

Instead of fasting entirely, she recommends someone who wants to do a detox regime could simply avoid sugar or processed foods for a period of time. This could involve eating a normal, healthy diet but abstaining from sugar or processed food. This won't be "damaging to the body the way these long-term fasts can be."

So why are these fad cleanses and flushes so popular? De la Forêt believes it's because "they have immediate results. People feel very different from them. They have instant gratification but long-term health problems." On the other hand, a healthy lifestyle provides slower, and much less drastic results, even though it is better for you in the long run.

Perhaps Marion Nestle, a professor of nutrition at New York University and author of many books including *What To Eat*, puts it best. She says, "Stay away from weird dietary practices. If they sound weird, they are."

9

Fad Diets Can Become Eating Disorders

Kathryn Diss

Kathryn Diss is a reporter specializing in business.

Many consumers try the latest fad diets in an attempt to lose weight quickly. Often, these diets result in unhealthy or disordered eating. Further, fad diets can be emotionally damaging, costly, and are generally ineffective for sustained weight loss. Dieters need to understand that becoming healthy means making the time to develop a healthy lifestyle. Trying to find a quick fix to weight problems can be dangerous.

When most people think of eating disorders, anorexia, bulimia and obesity tend to come to mind.

But there are many more eating disorders which people do not recognise as being a problem; from cutting out carbohydrates to only eating protein.

Health professionals say fad diets and eating trends can lead to obsessive disorders with unintended consequences for those on them.

They say the pressure to land a highly-paid job, work 60 hours a week, climb the corporate ladder, raise a family, hit the gym, and follow a strict diet all add to the problem.

"We live in a Fed-Exable society. It takes a year to gain weight, we want it off in one week," said health consultant Katherine Iscoe.

"It's a lot to do with restricting the amount of food we eat, and what we eat, and most of the time, it's eating too little, and also restricting food groups, the starchy carbohydrates, the refined sugars."

Brooke Rule has struggled to cope with eating normally since high school.

"If I'm not adhering to a strict diet or a strict set of rules then I'm not performing as well as I should and not being perfect like I think I should be," she said.

"I think it's really sad, the amount of hours you put into thinking about food and exercise and feeling guilty and bad then happy. I think it's sad there's a whole bunch of girls out there that feel that way."

While she has completed a medical degree and fully understands the science behind healthy eating, she has not been immune to social pressure.

From cutting out carbs to dropping five kilos in a week . . . it is all about a quick fix.

"I know that doesn't make any sense but I've still tried it because you can lose weight, you can be thinner if you cut out certain food groups, if you have a stricter diet, of course you're going to see a result," she said.

Fad Diets' Impact on Both Men and Women

WA [Western Australia] Dietician Julie Meek says fad diets do not only impact women.

"There's a lot of competition about how you look and it's not just women, it's men as well, that's from younger men through to older men," she said.

From cutting out carbs to dropping five kilos in a week, eating a high-protein diet to build muscle faster and hitting up the so called "superfood" of the month, it is all about a quick fix.

"It's like monkeys swinging through the trees, we grab one diet we swing on it for a while, again not being consistent, it's not really giving me the benefits I want, so we grab onto the next branch, try that next diet," said Ms Iscoe.

"Let's try the paleo, oh let's not eat anything, let's just have shakes all day, wait we're starting to gain weight again, let's swing to the next one."

Ms Iscoe said the fads are leading dieters towards destructive eating disorders.

"These are women that are beautiful, intelligent, that have careers but they feel they have to do more," she said.

"I personally think that has a lot to do with the impact of social media; Instagram, Facebook, and the pressures of everyone looking like a fitness model."

She said many people who struggle with food and diet issues do not believe they have a problem but they come to her because they are unhappy with their bodies.

"I try to dissect all their situations and try to attack each Lego piece, if you will, one at a time. Often by the end of it, they realise weight is not so important, I have so many other stresses to deal with," she said.

"It really depends on the extent to which you go on these diets.

"If you're restricting severely and restricting certain food groups, psychologically I think it's a slippery slope; it started at I'm not going to have any refined sugars, that soon after a few weeks develops into I'm not going to have any refined flours."

Julie Meek says they are very singular diets.

"That's what people tend to adopt if it says to take dairy, wheat and gluten out of my diet then I will, I'll take it out," she said.

"In the short-term that's not a real big problem but, in the long term, if they continue it, that has some massive effects on their health and wellbeing."

General Practitioners Are Not Able to Help

While Ms Iscoe mainly counsels women, Ms Meek says there are a growing number of men also developing unhealthy eating habits.

Ms Meek says their problems often go undiagnosed because they do not see the right health professionals.

"GPs [general practitioners] are so entirely overworked that they have such a short amount of time with people," she said.

"They also don't have the background to be able to deal with that so if you have a disordered eating pattern, if you're not referred onto a professional like a dietitian, you might actually just fall completely between the cracks."

Ms Rule eventually turned to Ms Iscoe's health program to help her understand where she was going wrong.

"She's really helped me cut through a lot of the excuses I had for why I wasn't living the life I wanted to live," she said.

"All those excuses about being too busy, she's really been able to see they were just excuses and now I've come up with solutions, and being able to recognise those thought patterns, and giving me ways to cope around that."

Health Department studies show Australians collectively spend up to $1 million a day on fad diets which have little impact on their weight and may be nutritionally unsafe.

And they are not only physically damaging.

"I think one of the biggest issues here is the mental side of it, because when you have issues with food that play on your mind all of the time, it's not a healthy relationship," said Ms Meek.

"And if you happen to be a mother of children and they are the habits that you yourself are doing, you're inadvertently passing them on to your children, you're setting up another generation of unhealthy eating."

For people like Ms Rule, recognising she had a problem was the first step to overcoming her disorder, a story she hopes will help others.

"My goals centre more about fitness than body type or shape any more," she said.

"So I have a goal to run the City to Surf [run in Australia], I have a goal to get stronger and to be able to lift more weights, I have a goal to eat healthy and to feel healthy with what I'm eating."

10

Diets Based on Appearance Are Dangerous

Jenny Chen

Jenny Chen is a science writer based in Washington, DC.

Dieting can be counterproductive as chronic dieters actually tend to consume more calories per day than people who don't diet. Further, the least effective diets are those driven by an obsession with one's appearance. In this case, dieters may stop paying attention to hunger and fullness cues. Research confirms that even casual attention given to appearance while eating can interfere with hunger cues and lead to overeating. Being aware of and responding to the body's messages on hunger and fullness can lead to a healthier diet and lifestyle.

Growing up I was terrified of being fat. My mother made disparaging remarks about girls on TV who were slightly chubby and the teen magazines I read were endlessly obsessed with losing weight. On the eve of my first year in college, I learned of the Freshman 15 in one of those teen magazines— the apparent inevitability that every freshman would gain 15 pounds in their first year in college. I was even more horrified when I arrived at school and found myself facing an endless buffet of desserts and cheese-filled entrees. I suddenly had to rely on my own self-control to stop myself from eating ice cream for breakfast. I didn't trust myself. I never had.

Dieting Out of Control

That's when I turned to the world of glossy fitness magazines and calorie counting. I put myself on a stricter and stricter diet of endless running and shrinking portion sizes. But that wasn't always enough—my body started rebelling with gnawing hunger and debilitating exhaustion. Whenever I felt like I was tempted to break my strict regime, I would turn to other people: I would look at people who were thinner than me as inspiration to get even thinner myself, and I would look at people who were bigger than me as inspiration for what not to look like. I became obsessed with appearances. One day I was changing in the morning when I caught a glimpse of myself in the mirror. The bones from my ribs and hips pushed softly from beneath my skin. I took a photo, in awe that my body was so different now from what it had ever looked like before.

Two years later though, things started getting out of control. I had lost so much weight that my advising dean wanted me to take time off of school. When I started trying to recover and eat more I found myself in a nightmarish spiral of binging and purging that I couldn't get out of. If I couldn't trust myself with food before, I was actually scared of food now.

New research may give a clue to how things spiraled out of my control, at least in part.

People who were distracted while eating were less likely to sense their body's internal satiety cues.

Fullness Cues

Researchers from the Netherlands published a study in the January 2015 issue of the *Journal of Experimental Social Psychology* that suggested that focusing on appearance could affect a person's sensitivity to their internal satiety cues.

"We found that focusing on how you look may hinder how you listen to your body's hunger fullness cues and how you adjust your food intake," said Evelien van de Veer, the paper's lead author.

Van de Veer and her team recruited 113 participants and conducted two experiments for their study. In the first experiment, researchers told participants they were participating in a milkshake taste test. They divided the participants into two groups. Both groups were given a milkshake to drink but only one group of participants had a mirror placed on their desk. Within each of these groups, half of the participants drank a high-calorie milkshake while the other half drank a low-calorie milkshake, but they were not told which one they were drinking. Fifteen minutes after the milkshake, the participants were asked to go into a room to watch a movie on a computer. There was a bowl of M&M's placed next to the computer. The researchers found that the participants who drank the high-calorie milkshake while looking at the mirror consistently ate more M&M's than the participants who drank the milkshake without looking into a mirror.

In the second experiment, researchers tested two groups of female participants. One group came before lunch (the "hungry condition") and the other half came after eating a filling lunch (the "satiety condition"). Half of the participants in each condition were asked to look at advertisements depicting thin models. They then participated in a cracker taste test, did 15 minutes of a filler task, and then the experimenter told the participants that she would leave the crackers on the table so that they could help themselves if they wanted to. While people in the "hungry condition" ate about the same amount of crackers whether they saw the models or not, research found that those who were in the "satiety condition" tended to eat more crackers if they had looked at the advertisements beforehand.

Researchers drew upon past research on self-objectification and distracted eating to explain why people in the experiments were less likely to sense fullness if they were focused on appearance. In a study from 2006, women who were preoccupied with how others perceived their bodies (a state psychologists call self-objectification) were more likely to be distracted and unable to focus on cognitively challenging tasks. Previous studies also found that people who were distracted while eating were less likely to sense their body's internal satiety cues. Thus, researchers suggested in the study that people did not adjust their intake according to fullness cues if they were focused on appearance because they were distracted from sensing those cues.

Chronic dieters also suffer from the negative impacts of focusing on appearance.

Van de Veer said that the experiment was unique because it tested how participants adjust their food intake over two separate episodes of consumption. "A lot of experiments look at the effects of external stimuli on one moment of consumption but we wanted to show there are effects [of focusing on appearance] from one moment to one moment. How you adjust what you eat from moment to moment is important because that makes up your total food intake," she said.

Jenni Schaefer, eating disorder activist and author of *Life Without Ed: How One Woman Declared Independence from Her Eating Disorder and How You Can Too*, says that this research confirms something that people in the eating-disorder community have known for a long time. "Sometimes you'll hear people with eating disorders say they're like a walking head. There's really no connection to their hunger and fullness cues," Schaefer said. "Looking back at my own eating disorder . . . I knew when I was really really hungry and I knew when I was really really really really stuffed. But I didn't know anything about those hunger fullness cues in between the far extremes."

Chronic Dieting and Change

But the research from the Netherlands doesn't just apply to people with eating disorders, said Evelyn Tribole, the registered dietitian and nutrition counselor who pioneered the Intuitive Eating program in 1996. Chronic dieters also suffer from the negative impacts of focusing on appearance. "I see this over and over again—people eat according to what they think celebrities or fitness models are eating," Tribole said. "Then they begin to ignore their hunger fullness cues and even stop feeling them after awhile."

Schaefer hopes that this research will prompt the dieting industry to help people break the cycle of endless dieting. "What's awesome about this study is that maybe the dieting industry will take note of this and help people make lifestyle changes as opposed to just going on diets, and change their marketing from being [based on appearance]," Schaefer said.

However, Evelyn Attia, director of the Center for Eating Disorders at Columbia University, says that it's unlikely that one study will inspire that kind of sweeping change.

"I don't think the verdict is out yet. I'd love to see the study replicated and tested across a variety of foods and images," she said. "If it turns out that the study can be further substantiated it begins to suggest that outside elements in our environment other than food affects our eating habits."

Organizations to Contact

The editors have compiled the following list of organizations concerned with the issues debated in this book. The descriptions are derived from materials provided by the organizations. All have publications or information available for interested readers. The list was compiled on the date of publication of the present volume; names, addresses, phone and fax numbers, and e-mail and Internet addresses may change. Be aware that many organizations take several weeks or longer to respond to inquiries, so allow as much time as possible.

Academy of Nutrition and Dietetics
120 S Riverside Plaza, Suite 2000, Chicago, IL   60606
(800) 877-1600
website: www.eatright.org

The Academy of Nutrition and Dietetics is the world's largest organization of food and nutrition professionals. The group strives to improve the nation's health and advance the profession of dietetics through research, education, and advocacy. The organization focuses on food and nutrition research and offers scholarships and awards. Its website, EatRight.org, contains numerous papers on managing a healthy, nutritionally sound vegetarian diet.

American Diabetes Association
1701 N Beauregard St., Alexandria, VA   22311
(800) 342-2383
e-mail: askADA@diabetes.org
website: www.diabetes.org

The American Diabetes Association funds research to prevent, cure, and manage diabetes. The organization's website includes basic information on diabetes, including descriptions of Type 1 and Type 2 diabetes, symptoms, statistics, common terms, health tips, and myths about diabetes. It also includes information on food, fitness, and lifestyle and how these factors influence the onset of diabetes in people.

American Heart Association (AHA)

7272 Greenville Ave., Dallas, TX 75231
(800) 242-8721
website: www.heart.org

The American Heart Association (AHA) engages in a range of activities, including medical research, professional education, and patient education, to promote a world free of heart disease and stroke. The AHA website provides nutritional guidelines and information on physical activity, stress, weight management, and smoking, as well as a section devoted to caffeine and heart disease.

American Society for Nutrition (ASN)

9650 Rockville Pike, Bethesda, MD 20814
(301) 634-7050
e-mail: info@nutrition.org
website: www.nutrition.org

The American Society for Nutrition (ASN) is a nonprofit organization dedicated to bringing together the world's top researchers, clinical nutritionists, and industry leaders to advance our knowledge and application of nutrition. ASN supports its members and fulfills its mission in a number of ways, including fostering and enhancing research in animal and human nutrition; providing opportunities for sharing, disseminating, and archiving peer-reviewed nutrition research results; and fostering quality education and training in nutrition.

Centers for Disease Control and Prevention (CDC)

1600 Clifton Rd., Atlanta, GA 30333
(800) 232-4636
website: www.cdc.gov

As the health protection agency of the United States, the Centers for Disease Control and Prevention (CDC) promotes health and the prevention of disease, injury, and disability. To accomplish this mission, the CDC conducts critical research and provides health information to members of the health-care and public safety community. The CDC website includes consumer health information on lifestyle diseases, such as heart disease and diabetes, as well as information about food safety and diet.

Health Canada

Tower A, Qualicum Towers, 2936 Baseline Rd.
Ottawa   K1A OK9
   Canada
(866) 225-0709
website: www.hc-sc.gc.ca

Health Canada is the federal department responsible for help-ing Canadians maintain and improve their health. Health Canada relies on high-quality scientific research and conducts ongoing consultations with Canadians to determine long-term health-care needs. Health Canada encourages Canadians to take an active role in their health and issues publications, in-cluding *Canada's Food Guide to Healthy Eating*, to advance this cause.

Health.gov

200 Independence Ave. SW, Washington, DC   20201
(877) 696-6775
website: http://health.gov

The Health.gov website, which publishes current dietary and physical activity guidelines for Americans, is coordinated by the Office of Disease Prevention and Health Promotion of the US Department of Health and Human Services. The website evaluates the strength of the evidence supporting each of the guidelines, provides detailed information on the nutrient con-tent of various foods, and also addresses issues like diet-related chronic diseases and food safety.

US Department of Agriculture, Center for Nutrition Policy and Promotion (CNPP)

3101 Park Center Dr., 10th Floor, Alexandria, VA   22302

(703) 305-7600
website: www.cnpp.usda.gov

The Center for Nutrition Policy and Promotion (CNPP), within the US Department of Agriculture (USDA), works to improve the health of Americans by developing and promoting dietary guidance that links scientific research to the nutrition needs of consumers. The agency's website includes considerable information on such topics as nutrition, dietary guidelines, USDA food plans, and other issues.

US Food and Drug Administration (FDA)

5100 Paint Branch Pkwy., College Park, MD   20740
(888) 463-6332
website: www.fda.gov

The US Food and Drug Administration (FDA) is the government agency responsible for ensuring the quality and safety of all food and drug products sold in the United States. As such, the FDA regulates safety and truthful labeling of all food products, including dietary supplements (except for livestock and poultry, which are regulated by the US Department of Agriculture), venison and other game meat, bottled water, food additives, and infant formulas. FDA reports, as well as current information on food quality issues, are available at its website.

World Health Organization (WHO)

Avenue Appia 20, Geneva 27   1211
  Switzerland
+41 22 791 21 11
website: www.who.int

The role of the World Health Organization (WHO) is to direct and coordinate international health within the United Nations' system. WHO supports countries by providing leadership, encouraging the dissemination of research, shaping and implementing standards, and providing technical support in efforts to coordinate their health systems, attain their health objectives, and support their national health policies and strategies. The WHO website offers a section on diet that provides links to activities, reports, publications, statistics, news, and events.

Bibliography

Books

Carrie Arnold — *Decoding Anorexia: How Breakthroughs in Science Offer Hope for Eating Disorders*. London: Routledge, 2012.

Charlotte Biltekoff — *Eating Right in America: The Cultural Politics of Food & Health*. Durham, NC: Duke University Press, 2013.

T. Colin Campbell — *Whole: Rethinking the Science of Nutrition*. Dallas, TX: BenBella, 2013.

Thomas Campbell and T. Colin Campbell — *The China Study: The Most Comprehensive Study of Nutrition Ever Conducted and the Startling Implications for Diet, Weight Loss, and Long-Term Health*. Dallas, TX: BenBella, 2006.

Robert J. Davis — *Coffee Is Good for You: From Vitamin C and Organic Foods to Low-Carb and Detox Diets, the Truth About Diet and Nutrition Claims*. New York: Perigee Trade, 2012.

Andreas Eenfeldt — *Low Carb, High Fat Food Revolution: Advice and Recipes to Improve Your Health and Reduce Your Weight*. New York: Skyhorse Publishing, 2014.

Matt Fitzgerald — *Diet Cults: The Surprising Fallacy at the Core of Nutrition Fads and a Guide to Healthy Eating for the Rest of Us*. New York: Pegasus, 2014.

Yoni Freedhoff   *The Diet Fix: Why Diets Fail and How to Make Yours Work.* New York: Harmony, 2014.

Malcolm Kendrick   *The Great Cholesterol Con: The Truth About What Really Causes Heart Disease and How to Avoid It.* London: John Blake, 2008.

Scott Kustes   *Processed in America: How the Food Industry Has Increased Obesity by Lowering Prices.* Venice, FL: Archangel Ink, 2015.

Alan Levinovitz   *The Gluten Lie and Other Myths About What You Eat.* New York: Regan Arts, 2015.

Woodson Merrell   *The Detox Prescription: Supercharge Your Health, Strip Away Pounds, and Eliminate the Toxins Within.* Emmaus, PA: Rodale, 2013.

Denise Minger   *Death by Food Pyramid: How Shoddy Science, Sketchy Politics and Shady Special Interests Have Ruined Our Health.* Malibu, CA: Primal Blueprint, 2014.

Robert L. Paarlberg   *Food Politics: What Everyone Needs to Know.* New York: Oxford University Press, 2010.

John Robbins   *The Food Revolution: How Your Diet Can Help Save Your Life and Our World.* San Francisco: Conari Press, 2010.

Eric Schlosser   *Fast Food Nation: The Dark Side of the All-American Meal.* Boston: Houghton Mifflin Harcourt, 2012.

Gary Taubes   *Good Calories, Bad Calories: Fats, Carbs, and the Controversial Science of Diet and Health.* New York: Anchor, 2008.

Nina Teicholz   *The Big Fat Surprise: Why Butter, Meat and Cheese Belong in a Healthy Diet.* New York: Simon & Schuster, 2015.

Melanie Warner   *Pandora's Lunchbox: How Processed Food Took Over the American Meal.* New York: Scribner, 2013.

Ari Whitten and   *The Low Carb Myth: Free Yourself
Wade Smith   from Carb Myths, and Discover the Secret Keys That Really Determine Your Health and Fat Loss Destiny.* Venice, FL: Archangel Ink, 2015.

Periodicals and Internet Sources

Anna Almendrala   "How 'Healthy Diets' Have Changed Over the Decade," *Huffington Post*, May 6, 2015. www.huffingtonpost .com.

Linda Bacon   "The Contrarian: Health at Any Size—Why Diets Are Harmful and Counterproductive," *Discover Magazine*, October 25, 2012.

Tracy Bowden

"Cancer Specialist Warns of Potentially Fatal Dangers of 'Miracle Cure' Fad Diets," ABC.net, March 30, 2015. www.abc.net.au.

Brian Cuban

"Eating Disorders Are Deadly, but Who's to Blame?," *LiveScience*, May 20, 2015. www.livescience.com.

Abby Ellin

"Juice Fasts. Paleo Diets. Organic Everything. What the Wellness World Is Selling Us May Be More than We Can Stomach," *New York Observer*, June 2, 2015.

Kris Gunnars

"10 Proven Health Benefits of Low-Carb and Ketogenic Diets," *Epoch Times*, June 2, 2015. www.theepochtimes.com.

James Hamblin

"Vegetarians and Their Superior Blood," *Atlantic*, February 24, 2014.

Angela Haupt

"HCG Diet Dangers: Is Fast Weight Loss Worth the Risk?," *U.S. News & World Report*, March 14, 2011.

Kathleen Jade

"Paleo Diet Benefits: Is It Worth the Switch?," *Mother Earth News*, October 1, 2013. www.motherearthnews.com.

Geoffrey Kabat

"Natural Does Not Mean Safe," *Slate*, November 26, 2012. www.slate.com.

Vivian Manning-Schaffel

"9 Unhealthy and Even Dangerous Diets," LiveStrong.com, January 19, 2015. www.livestrong.com.

Heather McClees   "The Effects of Too Much Animal
                   Protein on Our Liver," *One Green
                   Planet*, June 3, 2015.
                   www.onegreeenplanet.org.

Woodson Merrell   "The Real Reasons Juice Cleanses
                   Can Get Your Health Back on Track,"
                   Huffington Post, March 10, 2014.
                   www.huffingtonpost.com.

Bryan Miller   "How Crash Diets Harm Your
                   Health," Health.com, April 20, 2010.
                   www.health.com.

Rick Nauert   "Impulsivity Tied to Binge Eating,"
                   PsychCentral, May 25, 2015.
                   http://psychcentral.com.

Liz Neporent   "Dangerous Diet Trend: The Cotton
                   Ball Diet," ABCNews, November 21,
                   2013. http://abcnews.go.com.

Carl Nierenberg   "6 Potential Dangers of Juice
                   Cleanses and Liquid Diets,"
                   LiveScience, November 24, 2014.
                   www.livescience.com.

Corrie Pikul   "3 Diets That Do More Harm than
                   Good," *Huffington Post*, January 3,
                   2014. www.huffingtonpost.com.

Wesley J. Smith   "Vegetarians Less Healthy," *National
                   Review*, April 2, 2014.

Jacque Wilson   "Juicing: Healthy Detox or Diet
                   Trap?," CNN, April 11, 2014.
                   www.cnn.com.

Index

CPSIA information can be obtained
at www.ICGtesting.com
Printed in the USA
FFOW05n1911050116

9 780737 773958